Happy third birthday!
- Mr. William

God's Blessing!

A gift of love from:

_____

To:

_____

Acknowledgements

To all those who want to instill wholesome values to the children they love.

Dedication:

ISBN-13: 978-1544702261

ISBN-10: 1544702264

Mom! There's an Angel in the Kitchen!

by John Cappello

"Mom! There's an angel in the kitchen!" screamed little Max.

"Okay," shouted mom, shaking her head and smiling at the little man's comment. She thought it was so cute that he would think there was an angel in the kitchen. The thought quickly went away as mom went about her daily routine. After all, she had to get her housework done and head to work.

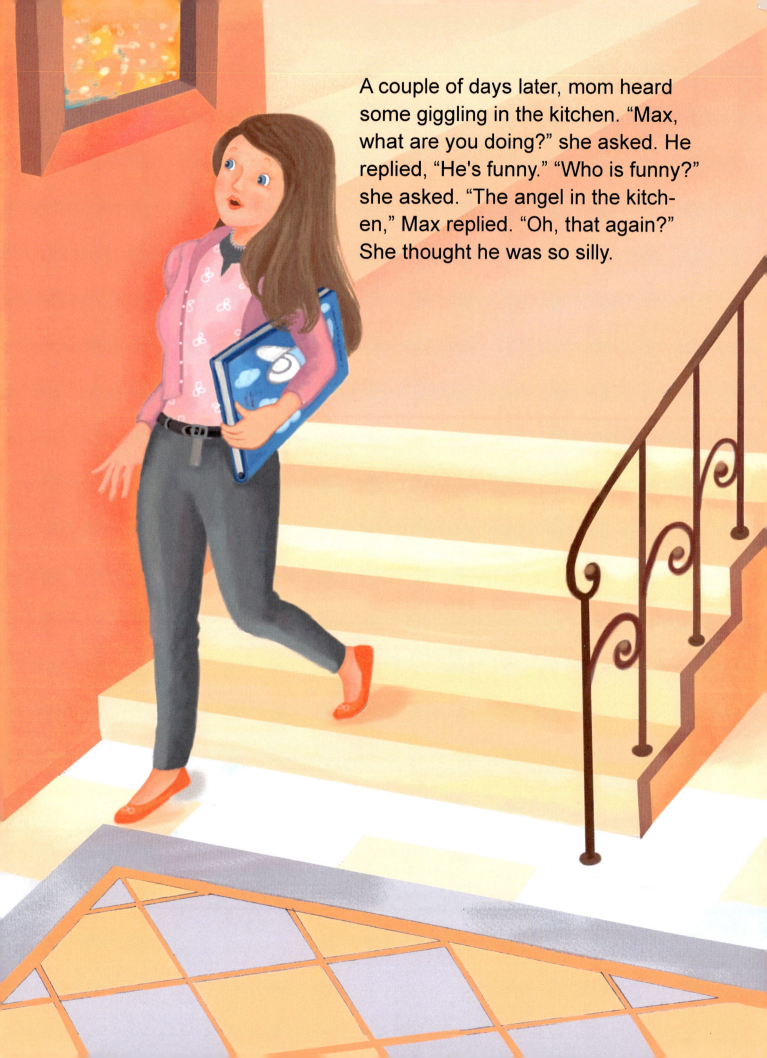

A couple of days later, mom heard some giggling in the kitchen. "Max, what are you doing?" she asked. He replied, "He's funny." "Who is funny?" she asked. "The angel in the kitchen," Max replied. "Oh, that again?" She thought he was so silly.

That same day, mom saw Jack, the family dog, wagging his tail like he was excited to see someone.

She thought, "That's strange. I wonder what is going on in the kitchen." She shrugged it off and thought maybe the dog saw a bug or one of his toys there. It wasn't anything to investigate.

A few more days passed, and mom and Max were alone at home. Max had just gone down for his afternoon nap when mom heard something in the kitchen. She wondered what was happening, so she ran to the kitchen where she saw an angel with huge wings standing there. She could not believe her eyes.

The angel turned around and greeted her. "You do not remember me, do you?" he said. "No, I do not," she replied. He said, "That's okay. Do you remember the poem you learned when you were a little girl?" She paused to think a moment and said, "I think I remember something like that." The angel continued, "Do you remember who gave you the poem?" Mom stood there a moment and suddenly remembered. "You gave me the poem," she cried. The angel said, "Yes. Do you remember the poem? It went like this."

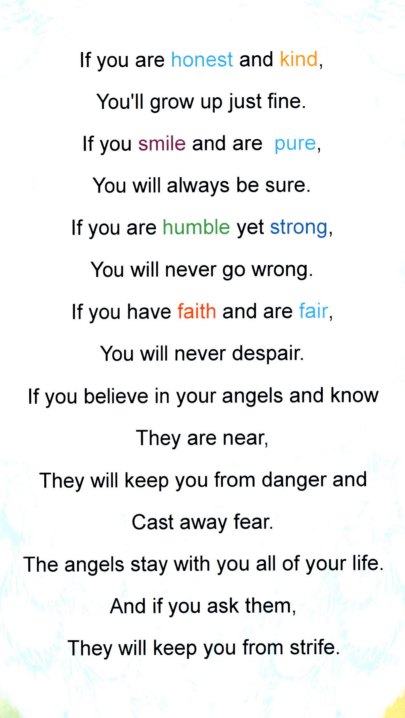

If you are honest and kind,

You'll grow up just fine.

If you smile and are pure,

You will always be sure.

If you are humble yet strong,

You will never go wrong.

If you have faith and are fair,

You will never despair.

If you believe in your angels and know

They are near,

They will keep you from danger and

Cast away fear.

The angels stay with you all of your life.

And if you ask them,

They will keep you from strife.

Mom remembered everything and realized these were words she had observed in her life since she was a child. She began to cry happy tears.

The angel was there to remind her of this poem and wanted her to share it with Max. "It is time for Max to learn these valuable words and use them in his life," the angel said.

Mom thought a moment and agreed that these wise words were helpful to her when she needed comfort or a boost of confidence. She decided that Max should learn them as well.

Max woke up from his nap and giggled at mom like he had always known about the poem and what it meant. It was like the angel and Max planned the whole thing.

Later that day, grandma came to visit. She heard mom and Max giggling in the kitchen. She asked her daughter, "What are you two giggling about? Max's mom answered, "Mom! There's an angel in the kitchen!"

The End

About the author

John Cappello is an award-winning self-help and metaphysical book author. He has an B. A. in Economics from the University of Dallas and an M. B. A. from the Graduate School of Management at the University of Dallas. He resides in North Texas with his family, two cats, and a dog!

Made in the USA
Lexington, KY
14 August 2017